## Verses From The UK

Edited By Sarah Waterhouse

First published in Great Britain in 2020 by:

Young Writers
Remus House
Coltsfoot Drive
Peterborough
PE2 9BF
Telephone: 01733 890066
Website: www.youngwriters.co.uk

All Rights Reserved
Book Design by Ashley Janson
© Copyright Contributors 2020
Softback ISBN 978-1-80015-019-5

Printed and bound in the UK by BookPrintingUK
Website: www.bookprintinguk.com
YB0446X

# **FOREWORD**

Here at Young Writers our defining aim is to promote the joys of reading and writing to children and young adults and we are committed to nurturing the creative talents of the next generation. By allowing them to see their own work in print we believe their confidence and love of creative writing will grow.

*Out Of This World* is our latest fantastic competition, specifically designed to encourage the writing skills of primary school children through the medium of poetry. From the high quality of entries received, it is clear that it really captured the imagination of all involved.

We are proud to present the resulting collection of poems that we are sure will amuse and inspire.

An absorbing insight into the imagination and thoughts of the young, we hope you will agree that this fantastic anthology is one to delight the whole family again and again.

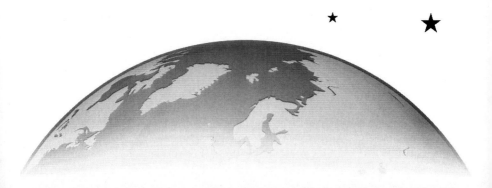

# CONTENTS

### Adel Primary School, Adel

| | |
|---|---|
| Aashaz Zia (8) | 1 |
| Leanna Elmussarah (7) | 2 |
| Clara Homes (8) | 3 |
| Xavier Percebois (8) | 4 |
| Joshua Davis (7) | 5 |
| Matilda Walsh (8) | 6 |
| Jacob Maxwell (7) | 7 |

### Arnold Lodge School, Leamington Spa

| | |
|---|---|
| William Ross (10) | 8 |
| Luca Davey (9) | 9 |
| Henry Bunting (9) | 10 |
| Aurelian Balboa (10) | 11 |
| Henry Savigar (11) | 12 |
| William Savigar (9) | 13 |
| Austin Mayhew (9) | 14 |
| Sophie Gordon (9) | 15 |

### Grange Park Primary School, Winchmore Hill

| | |
|---|---|
| Selin Derem (9) | 16 |
| Isaac Fields (9) | 17 |
| Aston Archer-Young (9) | 18 |
| Rhianna Mursal Faizy (9) | 19 |
| Perissa Patel (9) | 20 |
| Evren Okanay (9) | 21 |
| Matthew Allison (10) | 22 |
| Artin Heydari (10) | 23 |
| Keira Cheek (10) | 24 |
| Arabella Mumba (10) | 25 |
| Huseyin-Emre Denizer (10) | 26 |

| | |
|---|---|
| Gabriele Banelyte (10) | 27 |
| Flarjan Hafuzi (10) | 28 |
| Dino Mason (10) | 29 |

### Hasland Junior School, Hasland

| | |
|---|---|
| Ebony Johnson (11) | 30 |
| Olivia Ellwood (7) | 32 |
| Darlia Mann (8) | 33 |
| Ewan Wigfield (11) | 34 |

### Heamoor Community Primary School, Heamoor

| | |
|---|---|
| Lois Murrish (7) | 35 |
| Alexander Davy Eddy (8) | 36 |
| Sophia Davy Eddy (10) | 37 |
| Alexis Kearon (8) | 38 |

### Kestrel Class - Danesgate, York

| | |
|---|---|
| Mason Howes (8) | 39 |
| Max Widd (7) | 40 |
| Isaac Thackway (9) | 41 |
| Charlie Wood (8) | 42 |
| Harvey-Rai Gray-Harrison (7) | 43 |
| Oscar Wilson (10) | 44 |
| Ardem Safar (7) | 45 |

### Krishna Avanti Primary School, Evington

| | |
|---|---|
| Bhavani Nayee (9) | 46 |

## Millbrook Primary School, Grove

| | |
|---|---|
| Tia Golder (7) | 47 |

## Orston Primary School, Orston

| | |
|---|---|
| Florence Walters (9) | 48 |
| Theo Hallam Lees (9) | 50 |
| Erin Greensmith (10) | 51 |
| Lucy Taylor (10) | 52 |
| Violet Whitcher (10) | 53 |
| Missy Gleed (10) | 54 |

## OYY Lubavitch Girls' School, Salford

| | |
|---|---|
| Devorah Leah Kinn | 55 |

## Pitsford School, Pitsford

| | |
|---|---|
| Bella Suter (10) | 56 |
| Amelie Wilkins (9) | 57 |
| William Haynes (10) | 58 |
| Georgie Bennett (10) | 59 |
| Lucas Webb (10) | 60 |
| Darcy Burditt (9) | 61 |
| Evie Spray (10) | 62 |
| Agustin Hierling (10) | 63 |
| Bradley Richardson-Cheater (9) | 64 |

## St Bartholomew's CE Primary School, Stourport-On-Severn

| | |
|---|---|
| Jamie McAllister (10) | 65 |
| Rio Cherrington (10) | 66 |
| Miley Southern (10) | 67 |
| Damien Llewellyn (10) | 68 |

## St Chad's RC Primary School, South Norwood

| | |
|---|---|
| Pedro Onobhayedo (7) | 69 |
| Viola Bellagambi (8) | 70 |
| Emma Ifeatu Anene (8) | 74 |
| Leah (8) | 76 |

| | |
|---|---|
| Benjamin Katende (7) | 77 |

## St George's CE Primary School, Hyde

| | |
|---|---|
| Khadija Hussain (9) | 78 |
| Gracie Fidler (9) | 79 |
| Poppy Keegan (11) | 80 |
| Zainab Sheikh (10) | 81 |
| Mahika Echendou (8) | 82 |
| C Scott (10) | 83 |
| Daniyal Talukdar (8) | 84 |

## St Giles' & St George's CE Academy, Newcastle

| | |
|---|---|
| Layla Harding | 85 |
| Kelsey May Bradley (10) | 86 |
| Aaliyah Mohideen (9) | 88 |
| Scarlett Bird (9) | 89 |
| Sophia Grant (10) | 90 |
| Lucie Mayer (9) | 91 |
| Marietta Roberts (9) | 92 |
| Mark Jay Foster (9) | 93 |
| Tasha Siadjeu (9) | 94 |
| Ruby Jennings (9) | 95 |

## St Margaret Clitherow Catholic Primary School, Hanworth

| | |
|---|---|
| Evie Vincent (9) | 96 |
| Antos Stein (8) | 97 |
| Sofia Garcia-Audiche (9) | 98 |

## St Mark's CE Primary School, Swanage

| | |
|---|---|
| Jacob Peake (9) | 99 |
| Kaleb Fowler (9) | 100 |
| Katie Mae Kenny (3) | 101 |
| Lucas Cartridge (8) | 102 |
| Tilly Canning (8) | 103 |
| A-J Fear (9) | 104 |
| Ella Hardy (8) | 105 |
| Finley Stockley (8) | 106 |

## St Peter's Primary Academy, Easton

| | |
|---|---|
| Eleanor Elsie Miller (10) | 107 |
| Molly Kiddell (10) | 108 |
| Grace Louise Mills (11) | 110 |
| Livia Trett (10) | 112 |
| Imogen Rose Jarvis (10) | 113 |
| Taylor Osborne (10) | 114 |

## St Thomas Of Canterbury Catholic Primary School, Mitcham

| | |
|---|---|
| Karsten Dunkley (10) | 115 |
| Ihinosen Eboreime (9) | 116 |
| Chad-William Morris (10) | 120 |
| Francesca Marziano (9) | 122 |

## Upton Meadows Primary School, Upton

| | |
|---|---|
| Harvey Kirk-Smith (7) | 123 |
| Nehal Ba Omar (7) | 124 |
| Kira Newton (7) | 125 |
| Dexter Scott (7) | 126 |

## Whitehall Primary School, Whitehall

| | |
|---|---|
| Anouk Palmer-Moenks (11) | 127 |
| Freddie Liew (11) | 128 |
| Hamid Rana (11) | 130 |
| Solomon Endersby-King (11) | 132 |
| Lottie Nava (10) | 134 |
| Harri Snow (10) | 136 |
| Nathaniel Tsegaye (11) | 137 |
| Fern Rockett (10) | 138 |
| Ali Tariq (10) | 140 |
| Louis Parsons (11) & Bobby | 141 |
| Aiesha Wilkinson (10) | 142 |
| Alyssa Daveridge (11) | 143 |
| Nicole Jacquens (10) | 144 |
| Scarlett-May Gilpin Stone (11) | 145 |
| Méabh Maguire (10) | 146 |
| Amara Grandison (11) | 147 |

| | |
|---|---|
| Elena Olsen (11) | 148 |
| Elsa Roberton (11) | 149 |
| Iona Weaver-Brown (11) | 150 |
| Samira Hared (10) | 151 |
| Imran Mohamed (10) | 152 |
| Jude Jennings (10) | 153 |
| Riya Juttla (10) | 154 |

## Worsley Bridge Primary School, Beckenham

| | |
|---|---|
| Kayden Harris (11) | 155 |
| Amelia Butterly (10) | 156 |
| Caiden Walker (8) | 157 |
| Naomi Francis | 158 |

# THE POEMS

# Mathematics

M ultiplication is quite easy, but some questions are hard,
A lgebra is quite tricky for people who just learned,
T imes tables you learn up to twelve, but some people learn more,
H omework is extremely fun, especially maths for me,
E njoyable is an adjective I'd use to describe maths,
M ental calculations is the method for me, I really like to use it,
A ddition is so simple, it's the simplest for me,
T ricky is an adjective to describe some sums,
I ndices are tricky too, I'll give you an example, 15 to the power 18, the answer is colossal,
C alculations include addition and subtraction, also it includes multiplication and division,
S ubtraction is simple too, it's the second simplest for me.

**Aashaz Zia (8)**
Adel Primary School, Adel

# Guess Me

I'm dark, black, cute, small,
I can slide down hills in the sea
Of course I live in the Arctic as cold as can be
I may see the ice melting for me.
I'm living now in the freezing Arctic
I can hear the fish calling for me
I wish I were a pet but I cannot be.
It would be interesting to see Leeds.
Wow, if I were a pet seeing the humans see me!
I'm as slow as a waddling duck when I enter the sea.
Now there's a quiz, we can see if you know who I am.
Read this again and you will see
I want to tell you because I'm a...
Penguin!
Wow, how cool I know!
I'm clever, it's me!

**Leanna Elmussarah (7)**
Adel Primary School, Adel

# Magic

There was a girl called Lily
Who wondered if magic was true
Or if it was a myth.
I believe in it, do you?
Every night, she looked out of her window
Wishing for a pet unicorn.
"Magic is not real," she said.
She went to sleep.
She dreamed the best...

She was riding a unicorn!
She was swimming with mermaids and flying with fairies.
Cowboys came to capture them.
They were at the River Thames.
Lily rescued them.
"Hooray!" they all said.
She discovered that magic was true.
Just be yourself for you!

**Clara Homes (8)**
Adel Primary School, Adel

# Food

Scrumptious, delicious food.
Oh I know what I want
For it to be about food, yummy food.
No matter how hot or spicy food is
I'll still eat it!
Food can come in all shapes and sizes
Food can be rich, lovely, extraordinary, exciting
Food can be hot or cold but I'll still eat it
No matter the temperature.
I'll eat food.
What could be better than food hot or cold?
I would trade anything for food
Even a house or all my money just for food!
If food is cooking, I'd do something to shorten the time still
Just to eat food.

## Xavier Percebois (8)
Adel Primary School, Adel

# When I Grow Up

When I grow up, I want to be as tall as a white snowy mountain.
When I grow up, I want to be as fast as a speeding bullet.
When I grow up, I want to be as strong as a muscly, red-cloaked boxer.
When I grow up, I want to be as smart as a mathematics genius.
When I grow up, I want to be a book writer, selling books by the dozen.
When I grow up, I want to be a rich billionaire.

I can't wait to grow up!

**Joshua Davis (7)**
Adel Primary School, Adel

# Dream Land

In Dream Land, there is liquorice wrapped around the trees like a little girl's hair plaited.
In Dream Land, the waters are juicy.
In Dream Land, the king and queen are so strict, all their servants don't get anything.
In Dream Land, they have lots of candy to eat, in fact that's all they eat.
In Dream Land, the grass is as wiggly as a worm.
In Dream Land, is it real or a dream?

**Matilda Walsh (8)**
Adel Primary School, Adel

# Yellow

Yellow as bright as the sun.
Yellow as hard as lime stone.
Yellow like a star.
Yellow is a colour of the rainbow.
Yellow is all around Egypt.
Yellow is solid gold.
Yellow is as bitter as a zesty lemon.
Yellow is a colouring pencil.

If you look around, yellow is everywhere
In a house, on the wall and in a book.

## Jacob Maxwell (7)
Adel Primary School, Adel

# My Cat Marmaduke

My cat Marmaduke, he is ginger and white.
He chases string and tries to bite.
If you stroke him the wrong way,
He will get up and run away.

He pulls up our carpet with his claws
And tries to tunnel under our doors.
He can be very naughty,
Even though in cat years, he is nearly forty.

If we go out for the day,
He stays outside on his own to play.
He waits on the fence for us to come home
And makes us feel guilty for leaving him all alone.

He sleeps like a baby on my bed
And purrs really loudly when you tickle his head.

## William Ross (10)
Arnold Lodge School, Leamington Spa

# Monster!

Sneaking through the cemetery, never slain, never gone.
In the darkness it hides away from us.
The Devourer of Light, soul-snatcher, many names.
Wings stretching far out.
Gliding through the sky in the middle of the night.
Watch out! Behind you it sneaks.
Duck! Run! Hide away!
It's coming to get you!
This may be your end so run!
Goodbye...

**Luca Davey (9)**
Arnold Lodge School, Leamington Spa

# Haunted House

Walking down your street,
You stop on your two feet,
You come across a big dark house,
You see a hairy mouse,
You take a step towards the yard
And you see a small card,
On it someone had scribbled words,
For he wanted them to be heard:
'The loyal man who reads this, beware.'
You walk away...

## Henry Bunting (9)
Arnold Lodge School, Leamington Spa

# Haunted

Sleeping in your bed
Girl screaming
Something under your head
Floorboard creaking

Cupboard shaking
Bed swaying
I'm waiting
Zombies wailing!

Bones move like spiderwebs
Moving dolls
Vampire sped
Flying souls

Window closing shut
Bats eating dead bodies...

**Aurelian Balboa (10)**
Arnold Lodge School, Leamington Spa

# River

River so wide
River so long
River so beautiful
I hear your song.

Water so powerful
Water so strong
You'll pull me along
To the end of your song.

Ebbing and flowing
Not knowing where you are going
There by day, there by night,
Flowing from the darkness to bright.

## Henry Savigar (11)
Arnold Lodge School, Leamington Spa

# Poem

The boy was scared.
The boy was frightened.
The waves were round and pointy.
It was creepy.
It was scary.
As the boy sat on the black boat,
The lightning was loud and creepy.
The waves were strong and fearsome
As the boy wished he had never begun this journey.

**William Savigar (9)**
Arnold Lodge School, Leamington Spa

# Nintendo Switch

I am playing and I feel amused,
Cars and Zelda fiddle my mind,
They move and wiggle until they die,
It lets me into my own little world of freedom,
The data slowly downloads as I think,
The electric fizz of energy is the best thing to me,
It lets me think freely.

**Austin Mayhew (9)**
Arnold Lodge School, Leamington Spa

# Dogs

Dogs barking loudly like a fox.
Dogs are as soft as a cat.
Dogs playing football, in goal.
Dogs running fast like a cheetah.
Dogs are furry like a bunny.
Dogs are white, black and brown.
Dogs are cute like a bunny.
Dogs like cuddles like people.

**Sophie Gordon (9)**
Arnold Lodge School, Leamington Spa

# Murder Mystery

It was a day like any other in the city of LA. Except for the Kardashians.
"Where's the cake for Uncle Ben's birthday, Bella?" asked Giorgia.
"It's here!" Bella replied. Giorgia breathed a sigh of relief while hauling the cake into the car. Finally, after a couple of hours, they arrived at their destination. They joined the rest of the family on the yacht. Thankfully they weren't late. Once all the family were gathered together, the lights went out. *Bang!* There was a crash. There was shouting and confused murmuring. All of a sudden, the lights switched on.
Murder.

## Selin Derem (9)
Grange Park Primary School, Winchmore Hill

# Flash Saves The Day

Pete the truck driver, along with his husky Flash, had the anxious job of transporting a water pump across Australia to an isolated town. Unfortunately, the heavens opened and a deluge of water descended onto the only dirt road which provided access. The fifty-ton truck tyres became completely wedged into a sea of mud. Flash was struck by a bolt of lightning, giving him super strength. The husky held onto the tow rope securely with his jaws and pulled. Amazingly, the truck moved slowly at first but steadily, finally arriving at the warm welcome of the thirsty remote town's inhabitants.

## Isaac Fields (9)
Grange Park Primary School, Winchmore Hill

# Dragon World

A long, long, long time ago, there was a sinister dragon king called Ivan who went around deserted places like towns, villages and lots more. But there was also a good dragon king who went around saving other dragons, that also had a calm place with funny, smart and strong dragons. One day, the sinister dragon came to the good dragon's place to challenge the good dragon king to fight him for the throne. Three... two... one... fight! Both of them were clashing together.
"Argh!" screamed the sinister dragon. "You burnt my finger!" And the sinister dragon flew away.

**Aston Archer-Young (9)**
Grange Park Primary School, Winchmore Hill

# My Toy's Alive!

"Lucy! Dinner's ready!" Mum shouted.
"Okay! Coming!" I replied. As I dropped my doll down onto the floor of my boring, dull bedroom, I remembered wishing that my sister's fun, exciting bedroom was mine. Then, after I had eaten my dinner, I ran back up the stairs to see my pale-faced doll lurking around in the hallway. How could this be? Everyone in the house had been eating downstairs. I went back downstairs to get some more snacks to then find my doll lying down on my sister's bed. It could only mean one thing: my creepy toy was alive!

**Rhianna Mursal Faizy (9)**
Grange Park Primary School, Winchmore Hill

# The Child Who Couldn't Decide Who She Was

The girl felt alone. She didn't know who she really was. Was she a spy or was she a useless little brat? No. She was a secret spy. She took after her parents who were trained spies. She owned a cool cat that wore shades and had cloud-white fur. To top it off, it had a spy camera!
"Courtessa family, report to sir Smith's office immediately!" blared a voice from out of nowhere. Why oh why did she have to go? She felt like staying in her warm cosy bed. She couldn't be bothered. Reluctantly, she rose up...

**Perissa Patel (9)**
Grange Park Primary School, Winchmore Hill

# The Time Traveller

As I stepped into the dusty old TARDIS, not expecting anything bad, I set the year to 3000. As I went out and opened up my eyes, the sight was beautiful. Suddenly, a humongous ship came. "Leave this place now, or else!" I decided to go back into my TARDIS and went to gear 0, realising I could see Jesus' birth! As I climbed out, the beautiful baby was born. He had a gorgeous smile on his face. There was smiling everywhere too like it was Heaven. I decided to go back to 2020 so I went in the TARDIS and went home.

**Evren Okanay (9)**
Grange Park Primary School, Winchmore Hill

# Why Did Sam Kill Aoi?

There was blood on the floor. The detectives were searching the house. The murder had been committed. They had to find out who did it, what they did with it and why they did it. First, they had to find out who did it. Then they took our their magnifying glass and searched the building. They found out who killed Aoi, it was Sam. Next, they had to find out what he killed her with. They searched and searched. They found it under a broken floorboard, it was a butcher's knife. But they never knew why he killed her...

## Matthew Allison (10)
Grange Park Primary School, Winchmore Hill

# Emoji Land

Slowly, as I opened my eyes, I looked around and saw things that looked like emojis. Then I realised that they were emojis and how big they were... They were human-sized! I felt around for my legs and cautiously stood up. Then I peered up at some strangely shaped houses which had even more emojis. As I looked away, there were lots and lots of them staring carefully at me as if they had never seen such a thing. After some exploring, I started thinking of a name. I decided to call it Emoji Land. Only just for now.

**Artin Heydari (10)**
Grange Park Primary School, Winchmore Hill

# The Girl Who Cried Help

One day, a girl went out and cried, "Help!" Everyone came to see what was wrong, nothing happened. So the village went back to work. She did it five more times but they'd had enough.
The next day, the girl went to her grandma. She had to go through a forest. A rattle came from the bush, hissing was all she heard. It was a snake! She cried, "Help!" Nobody came because they thought it was a joke. The snake came closer. Without warning, she fell to the floor and never saw light again.

## Keira Cheek (10)
Grange Park Primary School, Winchmore Hill

# The Castle

I crept through the dark forest, hoping to find shelter. A bright flash of lightning appeared in the sky and it started pouring with rain. Soaking wet, with no shelter, I spotted a castle, I ran as fast as I could. I came to a big wooden door and knocked. The door swung open. I crept in and started exploring. Suddenly, I heard a noise and a door slam. Heading to where it had come from, frightened from head to toe, I opened the door... It was a ghost!
I woke up - phew, it was all just a dream!

**Arabella Mumba (10)**
Grange Park Primary School, Winchmore Hill

# Mike And The Unknown Phantoms!

Mike, who had a life-threatening disease, took a stroll in his local park. He noticed a tree flying in the far distance of the park. Mike went over and it morphed into a ghost! Mike found an abandoned house and sprinted as fast as he could go to the house. He shut the door with relief. As he thought the manic event was over with, he turned to find a gang of phantoms with soul-suckers! Mike had to call for help, although his voice was not on his side! Mike took a gulp and accepted fate...

## Huseyin-Emre Denizer (10)
Grange Park Primary School, Winchmore Hill

# Supergirl

One beautiful day, there was a girl named Emilya. She was walking along the seaside where she lived and surprisingly spotted a blue glowing necklace buried in the sand. She put it on and closed her eyes. Suddenly, she transformed into a superhero! She was blue, purple and pink! Every colour you could think of. A wonderful idea popped into her head. She could try and lift up her own house. That was exactly what she did, and it worked!

**Gabriele Banelyte (10)**
Grange Park Primary School, Winchmore Hill

# Super Spider-Man

I saw that Spider-Man was arresting the thief. After, he went to the police and he showed them the thief. Suddenly, there were more thieves coming. Spider-Man hid and the thieves came through the door with guns! Spider-Man jumped out at someone and he arrested him. The other thieves were walking away. Spider-Man arrested all of them. He went to the police and the police arrested them.

**Flarjan Hafuzi (10)**
Grange Park Primary School, Winchmore Hill

# The Search

In the pitch-black city, the spy was looking for its target. Blending in, he found his prey. In a split second, the target was off the street and on the floor, blinded.
Later on, the spy was waiting for his next target. Whatever happens, he is on the case...

**Dino Mason (10)**
Grange Park Primary School, Winchmore Hill

# The Space Spectacular

There are nine planets
That orbit the sun,
But people and animals
Live on just one.

The Earth is our planet
We must take good care,
With the air and water
That all people share.

The sun keeps us warm
Wherever we are,
All the light
Comes from this great big star.

A rocket is the best way
To travel in space,
With one great blast
You can go any place!

So when you sleep tonight
Look at the stars,

Maybe tomorrow
You'll be on Mars!

**Ebony Johnson (11)**
Hasland Junior School, Hasland

# Animals And Plants In Space

Look up to the sky!
I can't believe my eyes.
There is a flower up there
Next to a cloud shaped like a bear!
And what is that?
An apple tree with a bat.
He's trying to sleep.
But he doesn't know there is a fox about to leap.
What is this place?
There are animals in space!
There are plants in space.
What can we do?
What's that, a kangaroo?
And a mouse in his house!
Oh dear, oh no!
No one knows.
I can't wait to say -
The rock has a delay...

**Olivia Ellwood (7)**
Hasland Junior School, Hasland

# The Sparkle Planet

Have you ever heard of the Sparkle Planet? Well...

There once was a unicorn who travelled to space
And discovered the Sparkle Planet
It was the sparkliest planet she had ever seen

The unicorn glanced
And stared at the matter

She had found a face on it!
It had its tongue stuck out

It was so shiny that it blew her eyes out
And she lived on the Sparkle Planet forever!

**Darlia Mann (8)**
Hasland Junior School, Hasland

# Stars

Sometimes I wonder about the stars,
Is their big brother the red giant Mars?
Is the moon home
To giant space baboons?

How come space is endless?
How come it never ends?
It is out of this world.
It is literally out of this world.

I always thought black holes
Were full of coal.
When you adventure into the unknown,
Your adventure may never end.

**Ewan Wigfield (11)**
Hasland Junior School, Hasland

# Unitopia Planet

**U** nitopia is a magical place
**N** o one is bored here in space
**I** ndigo, violet and colours galore
**T** errific sights for all to explore
**O** ur planet is the best with its rainbow sky
**P** aradise for unicorns learning to fly
**I** ridescent wings shimmering in the sun
**A** ll day long they have so much fun!

**P** izza is banned as it makes unicorns fat
**L** ittle unicorns eat lots of KitKats
**A** nyone can come and visit for the day
**N** obody is allowed to eat their special hay
**E** nchanted creatures here and there
**T** here is also a forest of magic bears!

**Lois Murrish (7)**
Heamoor Community Primary School, Heamoor

# Journey Through Space

"All aboard the Mars Express to Pluto!" the alien captain shouts!
The aliens rush to find their seats as holiday time is beginning.
The spaceship blasts off into space.
The journey starts with a quick zoom around the sun,
Make sure you put your sunglasses on!
Mercury, Venus and Earth are next,
As the spaceship whizzes past.
Jupiter next, wow!
Watch out for the galaxy.
Hey! Does anyone want a quick spin around on Saturn's rings?
Uranus and Neptune coming up,
Please make sure you put your woolly hats on!
Now it's the final stop,
Please take all your stuff and enjoy your holiday on Pluto.

## Alexander Davy Eddy (8)
Heamoor Community Primary School, Heamoor

# Zombie Apocalypse

Z ombies
O MG!
M y my, nowhere to hide,
B ecause of an experiment
I don't like zombies
E verywhere

A ll around me,
P lease go away
O kay, who could I call for help?
C alling out to everyone
A round the world,
L ooking for a solution to end this nightmare
Y ippee! The solution is found
P ass it around,
S aving the world, so the zombies are...
E verywhere no more!

**Sophia Davy Eddy (10)**
Heamoor Community Primary School, Heamoor

# The Funny Alien

One day there was an alien called Bob who lived on Mars,
Bob tried to make friends but he got bullied,
But another alien said he was stupid!
So Bob went to school, he was lovely,
He told his mum and she said,
'Bob you are okay son!'
Bob made some friends
They were called Alex, William and Violet
They had fun, Bob's mum was glad!

## Alexis Kearon (8)
Heamoor Community Primary School, Heamoor

# Oh Crazy Space

Oh crazy space, oh crazy space
What about the human race?
And the planet Saturn's ring
Oh and I don't want to sing
And is Uranus blue or red?
I am dreaming in my bed
I know we live on big Earth
After I got given birth
I didn't know what was worth
But I'm now a big child
And I am not at all wild
And then there is Neptune
On Neptune, you will not find a balloon
And then there is the hot sun
But on there you won't toast a bun
Oh crazy space, oh crazy space
What about the human race?

**Mason Howes (8)**
Kestrel Class - Danesgate, York

# Pokémon Avengers Of The World

Pokémon flying through space
Floating in thin air
Pokémon peacefully sleeping in the rocket
Through the asteroid field they race
Pokémon running on the moon
Going home in the rocket soon
Flying around the Earth as quick as a cheetah
Raichu's skin as orange as the sun
Rayquaza's eyes as bright as the moon.

## Max Widd (7)
Kestrel Class - Danesgate, York

# The Survival

When I saw a shark as grey as a rock,
Sea like the sky,
Fish as red as blood.
A fish eating off a dish,
Making a wish for a bigger sea.
Coral like the Amazon forest,
Sharks swoop in as fast a cheetah,
Hungry for tropical fish
Whale as blue as water,
Saving fish.
The survival.

**Isaac Thackway (9)**
Kestrel Class - Danesgate, York

# The Deep

S harks scaring people
H unting for fish
A deep sea is where sharks hide keeping their mouths open
R ound the shark a human goes
K eep your eyes open so the shark doesn't see you.

## Charlie Wood (8)
Kestrel Class - Danesgate, York

# Fishing

**F** ishing on the Ouse
**I** n my wellies
**S** etting up my rod
**H** olding my reel
**I** can see the river
**N** ice! I caught a fish
**G** etting fish to release back into the river.

## Harvey-Rai Gray-Harrison (7)
Kestrel Class - Danesgate, York

# Kitten

**K** itten lying so cosy, as cute as a teddy
**I** love the tiger pattern on your back
**T** iny, baby-faced kitten
**T** ail so funny
**E** yes so crystal blue
**N** ose so black like night.

**Oscar Wilson (10)**
Kestrel Class - Danesgate, York

# The Mosasarous

**M** onsterous
**O** versized
**S** cary
**A** ngry
**S** caley
**A** ppears bigger
**U** gly ocean beast
**R** oaring
**U** gly
**S** harp teeth.

## Ardem Safar (7)
Kestrel Class - Danesgate, York

# This Is About Me

My name is Bhavani
And I am kind.
All of my poems
Came from my marvellous mind.

My favourite colour is blue.
I have got the best poems too!
I always love to write.
I always read when there is a light.

I have very long hair.
When I play a game, I'm always fair.
I love clothes that have feathers,
I also like shoes that are made from leather.

I really love my brother.
I've got the sweetest mother!

**Bhavani Nayee (9)**
Krishna Avanti Primary School, Evington

# Adorable Scruffy Piggy

Piggy is pink
Piggy is cheeky
Piggy is adorable
Piggy is floppy
Piggy is delightful
Piggy is stripy
Piggy is small
Piggy is cuddly
Piggy is soft.

**Tia Golder (7)**
Millbrook Primary School, Grove

# What Am I?

I bob about like bubbles in the sky,
But sometimes people make me into pie.
I tweet, I twoo, I yell and I squawk.
You cannot understand me but I can talk.
What am I?
Nobody knows,
But I might come and nibble your toes.

The bow I wear every day is pink,
If you see me, give me a wink!
I can't fly so don't expect me to,
My feet are too small to fit in a shoe.
What am I?
Nobody knows,
But I might come and nibble your toes.

I explore the planets but don't look for Mars,
I like to spend my time looking for chocolate bars.
You could say I zoom through space,
But I actually travel at a snail's pace.

What am I?
Did you get it right?
I am a hen... in space!

## Florence Walters (9)
Orston Primary School, Orston

# The Goners

We trudged all day through the sludgy mud
Our feet sank deep down into the ground
We were told that we were fighting for the greater good
As the guns blasted out their frightening sound.

The machine guns roared *a-rat-a-tat-tat*
Piercing bullets whizzed past like shimmers of light
"Quick, boys, run, we're under attack!"
White explosions lit up the black starless night.

All was quiet, then came the green gas
Drifting across the desolate no man's land
We struggled for our masks with frozen hands
Surrounding our souls like swaying grass.

Forever in my memory, these events will stay
As my little sister was born on Remembrance Sunday.

## Theo Hallam Lees (9)
Orston Primary School, Orston

# I Have A Pet Dragon

My dragon's really naughty
He runs around the park
He eats broccoli for dinner
And his middle name is Mark.

His next-door neighbour's Mary
Her legs are very hairy.
He flies around with birds
Though his calls are always heard.

The people in the town
Will never wear the crown
Because I have a pet dragon
And his pants are upside down.

**Erin Greensmith (10)**
Orston Primary School, Orston

# Out Of This World

In a world that is far far away, there are stars,
Further than Saturn, Jupiter and Mars.
This beauty is around us every day,
But we can't see them today
Because it is light
Though stars still shine bright.
So get out of your cars and look for stars,
Because their beauty is out of this world.

**Lucy Taylor (10)**
Orston Primary School, Orston

# Enter The Unknown!

Whooshing up, up and away,
Far beyond the Milky Way.
Stars shoot by as we fly
Among the planets in the sky.
Venus, Pluto, Jupiter, Mars,
Beyond the moon and past the stars.
Time for docking, going slow,
Hatch is open, in we go!
Weightless now, floating free
In this place of low gravity.

**Violet Whitcher (10)**
Orston Primary School, Orston

# Not That Different

Being the same
Not that different
Standing our ground
Not that different
Want to be normal
Not that different
Black skin
Not that different
Breaking down
Not that different
A little different
Still the same.

## Missy Gleed (10)
Orston Primary School, Orston

# Learning About Space!

The teacher said,
"Bring out your pen, ruler and writing books.
Now let us proceed with writing a poem in your book.
The title is 'Out of This World'!
Underline it with your pen and ruler.
Now let's start writing!"

Out of this world,
What can you see?
Some things look cool,
What can they be?
Sun, moon and stars,
Shining so bright,
Shining the world up in the night.

"Hand in your books one by one,
Sit back in your place.
Let's go on to the next subject
Which is maths!"

**Devorah Leah Kinn**
OYY Lubavitch Girls' School, Salford

# Asteroids

Search for them
In the dark depths of blackness
Capture them
In a magical notebook
Investigate them clearly
With the right mindset
A deadly skull of stillness
Waits to pounce.
Listen to the thump of your heart
That blood-curdling sound
Racing towards the Earth
Eventually
Coming to rest
Deep within the crust.

## Bella Suter (10)
Pitsford School, Pitsford

# Asteroids

Listen for them
In a cloak of darkness.
Capture them
In an eye of fire.
Seek them
In the never-ending bubble.
Investigate them
Through the largest telescope.
A rocky face
Filled with fear
Crashes down.
All hope is lost
As it smashes into Earth's sweet crust.

**Amelie Wilkins (9)**
Pitsford School, Pitsford

# Asteroids

Seize them
In the carpet of deepest black.
Store them
In the cupboard of wonders.
Examine their eyeless faces and ugly features,
Then banish them to the furthest corners of the rug of darkness.
Let them explore the other end of the room,
And make sure they never come back.

**William Haynes (10)**
Pitsford School, Pitsford

# Asteroids

Seize them
In the forest of gloom.
Capture them
From the jaws of a hungry lion.
Examine them
Through a mystical eye-piece.
A face -
Menacing in its shadows.
Seek what lies within its skull.
Reveal all its secrets.
Make it your own.

**Georgie Bennett (10)**
Pitsford School, Pitsford

# Asteroids

Detect them
In a cloak of darkness
Chase them
Through the mist.
Gritty and hollow-eyed
A spinning aroma of mischief.
A deadly, noiseless ball of rock
Strikes like a whip.
Cut open their hearts,
Seek what lies beneath the surface.

## Lucas Webb (10)
Pitsford School, Pitsford

# Asteroids

Listen for them
In a dark blue sea
Steal them
From a fisherman's net
Investigate them
Through a microscope
Look!
A hollow-eyed skull
Frightening and nightmarish.

**Darcy Burditt (9)**
Pitsford School, Pitsford

# Asteroids

Search for them
In a cloak of darkness.
Wrench them out
Of a dark cupboard.
Investigate them
When no one is looking.
Chilling in the blackest sky,
In search of death.

**Evie Spray (10)**
Pitsford School, Pitsford

# Asteroids

Grab them
In a pit of darkness
Reveal them from the dark.
Explore its inner faces
Dashing across the dusty sky towards Earth
A frightening sphere of rock approaches...

**Agustin Hierling (10)**
Pitsford School, Pitsford

# Asteroids

Listen for them in the darkest sky
Kidnap them from the deepest black hole
Examine them carefully
A gigantic villain sprinting into the unknown
Frightening in its destruction.

## Bradley Richardson-Cheater (9)
Pitsford School, Pitsford

# A Rocket Is...

A rocket is a car with wings
A rocket is a speed demon
A rocket is a slime as a train
A rocket is flashing and crashing
A rocket is a can of pop waiting to explode
A rocket is a colourful shooting star
A rocket is a hot radiator
A rocket is a tin full of Coke
A rocket is a blanket of fire
A rocket is a ball in the sky
A rocket is a fizzing explosion
A rocket is an arrow shooting across the sky
A rocket is an electric blanket
A rocket is a car exhaust
A rocket is a flaming bull
A rocket is a burning platform
A rocket is a tin of fire.

**Jamie McAllister (10)**
St Bartholomew's CE Primary School, Stourport-On-Severn

# What's Up In Space?

Rockets going into space like the
speed of lightning,
The black hole is dangerous, you can get
lost in time.
The Milky Way galaxy has over 10 billion stars
dancing across the universe,
The moon is as dusty as an
abandoned, haunted house.
Pluto is the furthest away from the red-hot sun,
Meaning it's the last to rotate the
yellow ball of lava.
Jupiter is the planet made from space rocks,
Which clump together like dough.
All the planets in the universe orbit the sun
At different times making them all unique.

### Rio Cherrington (10)
St Bartholomew's CE Primary School, Stourport-On-Severn

# Pretty Pink Aliens

Up in the sky are pretty pink magical aliens,
That make potions that change the world,
They have sleepovers so they can think
about their missions,
Their names are Beauty, Candy and Magical,
Their planet is made out of food and candy,
One of their most important missions was to catch
a shooting star,
But they failed, but if they don't catch it soon it will
be ruined,
But if they don't be careful if will take their powers,
They want to catch it so it doesn't
take anyone's powers.

### Miley Southern (10)
St Bartholomew's CE Primary School, Stourport-On-Severn

# What Does An Alien Do?

An alien flies
An alien lies
An alien spells
An alien smells
An alien jumps
An alien bumps
An alien floats
An alien hopes
An alien rides
An alien hides
An alien eats
An alien beats

An alien is a special creature!

## Damien Llewellyn (10)
St Bartholomew's CE Primary School, Stourport-On-Severn

# Sonic X

Sonic is very fast
He lives with Chris so everything is first class
He is a blue hedgehog the size of my knees
Every time he runs he shouts "Wee-hee!"
He leaves a blue trail wherever he goes
He has small ears and a tiny nose
He looks the same as a figure called Shadow
He got on earth by using Chaos Control
His rival is Doctor Eggman
He also has a lot of fans
Not the fans that blow you away
The fans that adore you in a good kind of way!
Sonic has a good friend called Tails
Who can build a clock that can chime
He has a girlfriend called Amy
Who chases him around all the time.

**Pedro Onobhayedo (7)**
St Chad's RC Primary School, South Norwood

# A Boy Who Loves To Rhyme

Once there was a little boy who loved to rhyme
But his parents told him he was just wasting his time
In the old, crinkly car the boy was going to school
All of a sudden they ran out of fuel!

They screamed in agony for help
Soon to the rescue came their kind friend Delp
The little boy said, "Hello!
I have a brother called Bello."

"Why in the world are you rhyming?
Also, the other day you were spying!"
He felt very ashamed
Also his parents didn't give him a name.

His teacher always calls him 'you'
But one day a loving friend said to the teacher, "Boo!

We don't have to be mean as he doesn't have a name
We should always treat people the same."

"You should go to detention
Don't even mention
'Cause I don't want your aggression
Just your perfection.

You can stay there for two hours
Let's see your special powers
You always laugh
And for years never taken a bath."

Wendy came to his house
They played a game called Mouse
"Can I call you kind friend
Because I never want this friendship to end.

I like your rhyming
Remember when our teacher was whining
Can you tell me some amazing rhyming words?"
"Alright... bat and bird!

Day and night they're always tweeting
Some days they are sleeping."
"That is amazing, better than good!"
The boy said, "I learnt it from a book."

He is a smart, intelligent boy
And he is full of joy
One day he felt sick
His dad told him to get up quick.

Then he saw a little baby thing
What bad luck did God bring?
He was turning into a bird
He felt he wanted to eat dirt.

He had a beak growing
All of a sudden he was blowing
Out of the blue, he was flying high
He took off and said, "Bye-bye!"

Once there was a little boy who loved to rhyme
But his parents told him is he was wasting his time
He flew to France, Africa and everywhere
His parents didn't even know he wasn't there.

He will never tell his secret to his friend
So my poem has come to an end.

## Viola Bellagambi (8)
St Chad's RC Primary School, South Norwood

# The Forgotten Forest

Comfortably we are, lack we never
Comfortably we lay as good animals
Sleeping and dining together always
Our thick forest flourishing with milk and honey
It's home sweet home
One summer fate struck
The arrow of scorching heat from the equator
Pierced through the heart of the beautiful forest
Tragedy we never knew
Our forest, our home, burnt down
By scorching heat
Homeless we became
Our home, the forgotten forest
In search of refuge
Trekking on, all the way
On route to the unknown
With the horizon staring in our faces
In the North Pole
We found ourselves
So cold, so chilly, no forest
Desperate for food and shelter

A miracle came to pass
And climate change befell the icy land
The soil became tropical
And once again
A thick forest came to life
And we could smile again.

## Emma Ifeatu Anene (8)
St Chad's RC Primary School, South Norwood

# The Coming Of The Iron Man

The Iron Man stood on the brink of the cliffs,
Tall as a house, all rigid and stiff.
His great iron head turned left then right,
As he stood on the cliff in the dark of night.
His headlamp eyes searched far and wide,
His iron ears listened to the swell of the tide.
Where had he come from, no one knows,
But there on the cliff where the seagulls rose,
The Iron Man stood with the wind in his face,
Then he lifted a foot and stepped into space.
Crashing, crashing, thrown about,
Til his legs fell off and his eyes fell out.

**Leah (8)**
St Chad's RC Primary School, South Norwood

# The War Zone

As I looked up in the sky,
The planes flew by,
The planes were as high as a kite,
I heard the wild engines cry,
I sighed.
It was as loud as a rocketship,
I gripped on to my teddy bear,
I couldn't bear the noise anymore.
I looked to the floor,
I saw the green grass waving back and forth,
A bomb had just exploded,
In the distance the enemies loaded guns,
I realised I was in a war zone,
I felt like running,
But my legs were stuck to the floor.

## Benjamin Katende (7)
St Chad's RC Primary School, South Norwood

# Dreamland

I see twinkling stars glistening in the midnight sky,
I hear the soft, whimsical music whispering
through my ears,
I taste the amazing honey
from the beautiful lavender,
I feel the glowing stars shimmer on my hands,
I smell the different types of chocolate
that fill the air,
I see dark blue flowers blossom all around me,
I hear the soft splashes of a dolphin,
I taste the raindrops that come shooting down,
I feel the warm breeze slither through my skin,
I smell the wonderful smell of sushi.

## Khadija Hussain (9)
St George's CE Primary School, Hyde

# Dreamland

I see twirling navy planets in the midnight sky,
I smell cheese from the moon,
It looks like the sunshine,
I hear aliens having a confusing conversation,
I taste sweet chocolate
All the way from Planet Mars,
I feel the roasting hot, honey-coloured sun
on my skin,
This is my dreamland and I hope it is yours too!

**Gracie Fidler (9)**
St George's CE Primary School, Hyde

# Mythical Dreams

I smell sweet lollipops
I hear calm music
I see the crisp snow
I taste golden caramel
I feel the breezy wind
I smell the deep sea
I hear the unicorns from nearby
I see the moonlight sparkle in the sky
I taste the chocolate river
I feel the soft grass.
I awake.
The dream is out of grasp.

**Poppy Keegan (11)**
St George's CE Primary School, Hyde

# Dreamland

I see the emerald sea glimmering like the moon,
I hear animals coming and going so soon,
I smell cotton candy from the air,
I feel the golden floor with my feet everywhere
I taste the food fifty times better than on Earth
I love Dreamland
I wish it was the place of my birth.

**Zainab Sheikh (10)**
St George's CE Primary School, Hyde

# Candyland

I see colourful, delicious candy everywhere
I feel squishy and white marshmallows
as I sleep
I smell fresh rainbow cake
I hear chestnut birds singing
I taste yummy lollipops.

### Mahika Echendou (8)
St George's CE Primary School, Hyde

# Rainbow Dreamland

I see golden daffodils
I hear candyfloss birds cheeping a relaxing song
I taste scarlet apples in the air
I feel the rainbow unicorns
I smell amber apricots.

## C Scott (10)
St George's CE Primary School, Hyde

# Golden World

I see the golden sky
I have billions of pounds
I see ocean clouds
I smell candyfloss in the river
I taste strawberries.

**Daniyal Talukdar (8)**
St George's CE Primary School, Hyde

# The Moon

My dream of going to the moon,
Soaring threw the darkest room,
Seeing the sun blind me at noon,
I'd love to see it all come true,
With guarding planets all around,
As space feels like home!
Floating around the atmosphere
The stars shine bright
And blinds my eyes
Loving the dream inside of me!
I pass the guardians of space
Soar around the darkest place
Never lights always dark in this base
Will I ever see this place?
My dream of going to the moon
Is now coming true
As I train, it becomes more true
My dream of going to the moon
Is finally coming true!

**Layla Harding**
St Giles' & St George's CE Academy, Newcastle

# My Alien Front

As I sit in my rocket and head up to space,
I'm excited but thinking about the place,
Up we go higher and high,
The crazy things you see when you're high in the sky.

Spaceships, planets, stars and all,
But the greatest one of all is my friend Paul,
He's green and slimy, a bit scary to see
But I like him, he's my friend and he likes me.

I put on my spacesuit and get out my rocket,
Looking for my friend with some sweets in my pocket,
When I find him we go for a tour,
Visiting each planet, some I like more.

Uranus, Jupiter, Saturn and Mars,
All these are beautiful especially stars,
Jumping, floating, high in the sky,
I love it in space, I can really fly.

The time has come I need to get home,
So I in my rocket and sit on my throne,
I wave goodbye to Paul until I see you,
Again take care, my good friend
And my rocket then flies.

## Kelsey May Bradley (10)
St Giles' & St George's CE Academy, Newcastle

# The Space Attack

As the sun set, Starmoon awoke. Along came Super Space trying to avoid her star laser. She flew across the sky like a beautiful butterfly, fluttering her owl wings around Starmoon's spacey outfit. Then the drama began... *Whoosh!* Starmoon lifted her speedy hands and obnoxiously pushed wind towards Super Space. The wind is stronger than fire but softer than water. This made Super Space angry. *Crash!* Super Space increased her water blaster and blasted it at Starmoon.
Now they are both angry! Both girls landed back on their planets.

## Aaliyah Mohideen (9)
St Giles' & St George's CE Academy, Newcastle

# Race In Space

In a dark, dark part of space
We were about to start a race
From Pluto to Mars, along the Milky Way
With no one getting in my way.
Through black holes and wormholes, flying at pace
I was thinking to myself, *I'm going to win this race*
Swerving to the left and turning to the right
Going around the corner I saw a wonderful sight...
*The finishing line!*
The trophy is now all mine.

## Scarlett Bird (9)
St Giles' & St George's CE Academy, Newcastle

# Planets

One day I would like to see the Milky Way,
why don't we start today?

In our rocket we will zoom,
until I see the gleaming moon.

Out the craft we shall go,
floating like we are in slow-mo.

The Earth from here looks very small,
almost like a toy football.

The sky is a carpet of sparkle and shimmer
But I better get home now for my dinner.

**Sophia Grant (10)**
St Giles' & St George's CE Academy, Newcastle

# The Alien That Lives On The Moon

I am an alien out of space
I look like you with a funnier face
I live on the moon
So come and visit me soon
I can see all the planets
They look so dynamic
My favourite food is pomegranate
I sit on the moon
Whistling my tune
Halley's comet go zoom, zoom, zoom
So like I said, I'm sat on the moon
So you are than welcome to come see me soon!

**Lucie Mayer (9)**
St Giles' & St George's CE Academy, Newcastle

# Moon In The Night

Oh moon in the night,
Shall it be,
Will I ever get to,
Go to the moon and back?

Maybe I am just exaggerating
Moon in the galaxy
Please, please let me
Shall I go to the moon and back?

Or shall I not go?
To your glorious, shiny moon
Like silver necklaces
It is your decision.

Shall it be me,
Or shall it be another?

**Marietta Roberts (9)**
St Giles' & St George's CE Academy, Newcastle

# Neil Armstrong

Neil Armstrong is the bravest man who ever lived,
He is as brave as a lion,
To get the flag and put it on the moon,
It couldn't have happened to just anyone,
My nana Carol couldn't have gone to the moon.
At the age of 16, she printed cups
Of Neil Armstrong planting the flag instead.

**Mark Jay Foster (9)**
St Giles' & St George's CE Academy, Newcastle

# It's A Blast

Put on your spacesuit
We're going to the moon
So make sure you're ready
We're going to blast off soon
Make sure you're comfortable
Strap yourself in tight
Say one last bye-bye
Get ready for the flight
3, 2, 1... off we go!

**Tasha Siadjeu (9)**
St Giles' & St George's CE Academy, Newcastle

# Aeis

Up in space there are a lot of surprises
Like aliens of all shapes and sizes
If you were in the galaxy with stars
You might see Mars
In a galaxy far far away
There lies the Milky Way.

**Ruby Jennings (9)**
St Giles' & St George's CE Academy, Newcastle

# The Dream!

In my dream,
I'm in the sea floating,
Floating wild and free,
Turtles, dolphins, fish and whales,
Fishing boats with windy sails,
Dolphins splashing, turtles flapping,
Seagulls flying past,
In my dream, I am far away,
The magic always lasts.

In my dream, the whales sing
A haunting melody,
The gentle giants of the sea
Are calling to me,
The turtles swim like floating rocks,
Avoiding stingrays with their frightful shocks,
The sun is hot,
The sun is bright,
As the day turns into night,
The sun retreats behind the sea
And in my dream, there's only me.

### Evie Vincent (9)
St Margaret Clitherow Catholic Primary School, Hanworth

# Bath

Once I was in the bath
In half of it,
Then suddenly, the plug burst!
First, it sucked me in,
Into a place I've never been,
It was called Ryn!
There were loads of bins
And creatures called Hyns!
I wanted to climb a height,
And then I realised, I don't have the right,
To climb to a very tall height,
So I climbed a small one or two,
Get a good view of the pathetic Hyns,
I saw they had 12 eyes and ate flies!
Now as the adventure ends,
The path bends,
I walk and find myself in the bath,
That's half, I was finished washing.

## Antos Stein (8)
St Margaret Clitherow Catholic Primary School, Hanworth

# It Wasn't Me

She did it, why would you blame me?
I just tried to make things right,
Oh please give me a cup of tea.
I'm using all my strength and might.

The pencil broke itself,
And the ruler fell off the shelf,
It wasn't me, it wasn't me,
I swear it was the elf!

**Sofia Garcia-Audiche (9)**
St Margaret Clitherow Catholic Primary School, Hanworth

# Humans

Beavers live in and build dams,
But humans make them go ka-bam!

Scientists are going to block out the sun,
Trying to steal our summer sun.

Plastic bottles fill the sea
Causing sea creatures' misery.

Clearing the Amazon to make room for cattle
Is Mother Nature's greatest battle.

Fossil fuel poisons the air,
Do most humans even care?

Australia burnt and the Arctic melts,
Is this the hand that we've been dealt?

**Jacob Peake (9)**
St Mark's CE Primary School, Swanage

# My Dream

Playing football is the love of my life,
I'd rather marry a ball than a real wife,
I'd take the field to fulfil my dream,
Which is to play for Man Utd football team,
They'd give me the ball for me to score,
And I'd listen to the crowd give a mighty roar,
One day I'll have people asking to sign my name,
To go with all my fortune and fame,
All I want to do is succeed,
Just one chance is all I need.

**Kaleb Fowler (9)**
St Mark's CE Primary School, Swanage

# Wicked Witches

Wicked witches are horrible,
They are like a dirty rat,
She doesn't look adorable
She always has her cat.

She has an old flying broomstick,
She holds it with her hands,
We can believe she'll never kick,
She could've joined some bands.

She always has her hat on,
We might know she can snatch,
We all know where she comes from,
There are potions she should catch.

**Katie Mae Kenny (3)**
St Mark's CE Primary School, Swanage

# My Worst Nightmare

It was dark
It was scary
There were cracking floors
Creaking doors
Spooky, spooky
It was spooky
It was foggy
There was dark grey fog
A big brown bog
Oh no, who is here?
It was cloudy
It was stormy
There were spooky clouds
Dark blue skies
Too many spooky nights.

**Lucas Cartridge (8)**
St Mark's CE Primary School, Swanage

# Different Dogs!

Big dogs, little dogs,
Wagging their tails,
Big dogs, little dogs,
Either bark or wail,
Big dogs, little dogs,
Hunting for a bone,
Big dogs, little dogs,
Snuggled up at home,
Big dogs, little dogs,
All crazy and daft!
Big dogs, little dogs,
Hate taking baths!

**Tilly Canning (8)**
St Mark's CE Primary School, Swanage

# Bubbles

Bubbles, bubbles
All sorts of troubles
Bubbles, bubbles
*Pop! Pop! Pop!*
Bubbles, bubbles
Big bubbles, small bubbles, fun bubbles
Bubbles, bubbles
Cool bubbles!
Bubbles, bubbles
Where do they go?
Bubbles, bubbles
Nobody knows!

## A-J Fear (9)
St Mark's CE Primary School, Swanage

# Illusionist

It's amazing
Looking with astonishment
Looking wonderful
Unbelievable!
So beautiful!
It was as shiny as a disco ball
Oh no!
No! That is amazing!
It was magical
Somersaults are amazing
Thank you!

**Ella Hardy (8)**
St Mark's CE Primary School, Swanage

# Getting A Kitten

*A limerick*

Once there was a kitten called Maggy,
Her hair was smooth and shabby,
I saw four kittens in a cage,
They just looked the right age,
But none of them were Maggy.

**Finley Stockley (8)**
St Mark's CE Primary School, Swanage

# Sun, Moon And Stars

In the black of night I gaze above,
The stars are shining down with love,
Near and far, large and small,
Twinkling bright, they watch us all.

When I have lost the way to go,
The moonlight guides me down below,
Crescent-shaped or full and round,
Beaming down upon the ground.

Happy and joyful I can be,
When the sun is shining down on me,
Rising up to start my day,
Brings light and warmth in every way.

When the sun sets and goes to bed,
I know it's time to rest my head,
The moon and stars are gleaming bright,
When daytime ends and turns to night.

**Eleanor Elsie Miller (10)**
St Peter's Primary Academy, Easton

# A Space Adventure

A lot higher than the sky,
There's lots of places I can hide.

Up, up and away I go,
Fly away just like a crow.

I see a spaceman in his rocket,
I turn around and see a comet.

I fly deeper into space
And look around, I see a face.

I feel happy yet confused,
I am excited and amused.

I see the face, bright eyes like stars,
I see the nose as red as Mars.

I turn my head and quickly steer,
I turn back and it disappears.

I turn back around to Earth
And sat down in my place of birth.

I hear a noise, loud and long,
My mind goes blank but my mind's strong.

I open my eyes and see my room,
I know it was a dream but one I won't forget soon.

Back in my room, I'm safe and warm,
But I never forgot that magical dream form.

## Molly Kiddell (10)
St Peter's Primary Academy, Easton

# Our Galaxy, Our World

Our galaxy, one of a kind,
Beyond the world of my mind.
Jet-black, brilliant blue,
Crystal white and purple too.
Home to so many radiant stars,
As far as the ones right near Mars.

All eight planets have their place,
Together in this ink-black space,
Two hundred moons in orbit,
Hooked together like a bracelet,
Mercury, Venus, Earth and Mars,
Jupiter and Saturn aren't last,
Uranus and Neptune are so cold,
They are the last but not all.

Our planet, different to the rest,
Has human life as its guest,
Life is known on epic Earth,
All since the sudden birth,
Day and night, light and dark,
All started with a big, bright spark.

Our galaxy, our world,
We only have one so spread the word.

**Grace Louise Mills (11)**
St Peter's Primary Academy, Easton

# Shooting Star

S hooting through the universe
H iding all over
O ut of the world totally
O MG can you see the glittery star
T ime to see it fly
I t is shooting, flying and sashaying all around the universe
N ow it is slowing down and getting more glitzy
G etting even faster... *whoosh!*

S hooting everywhere with a big explosion of sparkles and colour
T ime to watch the sparkles disappear into the universe
A nd guess what, it just flew over Planet Earth
R eady, steady, slow down...

*Shooting star!*

## Livia Trett (10)
St Peter's Primary Academy, Easton

# The Shadows From The Galactic Galaxy

As I woke up from a dream,
I could see a galactic gleam.
The stars are working together,
To make a luxurious galaxy of colours.
They all worked well as a team.
As I looked around my room,
I could see shadows coloured
In blue, pink and purple.
Then I heard voices saying,
"We're your Galactic Galaxy Team,
And we're here to build your dream!"
"Galaxies and stars will twinkle in the sky."
As I heard that I drifted back to sleep,
And dreamt of stars twinkling in the sky.
I'm delighted to have my very own Galactic Galaxy Team!

**Imogen Rose Jarvis (10)**
St Peter's Primary Academy, Easton

# The Wind

The wind is playing autumn games,
Through the gardens and the lanes,
The wind is ghostly because you can't see it,
The wind is invisible and it's as cold as ice in winter,
The wind is cool in summer,
The wind is the leaves' best friend as they fly through the air like a rocket going to the moon,
The wind is as funny as a very funny person as the wind tells the leaves jokes.

## Taylor Osborne (10)
St Peter's Primary Academy, Easton

# My Feelings

As tears drop from eye to eye,
I remember the things we used to do...
I remember
My feelings.
I see them saying hello and goodbye...
My feelings.
The smile on their face,
The hello and goodbye.
As tears drop from eye to eye,
I just can't say goodbye.
Don't leave me...
Don't go.

**Karsten Dunkley (10)**
St Thomas Of Canterbury Catholic Primary School, Mitcham

# The Uninvited Creature

In the darkest depths of the night,
During the storm and thunder,
I opened my murky door
Not knowing I would blunder.

But down the dreary doorway,
I heard a cry and felt myself stiffen,
I continued to creep forward shakily,
Until I came face to face with the griffin!

When I focused my sight,
It was illuminating the place with fire,
Its beak shone and its wings were sleek,
That was something to admire.

I couldn't make it move,
I couldn't make it stay,
This thing did as it pleased
As I imagined my mother's dismay...

I snapped back to my senses,
I knew my family would soon be awake,

What would happen if they saw this?
Should I tell them it was a fake?

I panicked, sinking to my knees,
The griffin looked concerned too,
I couldn't keep it in my house,
No one will accept it... would you?

What choice did I have?
Who would believe me too?
If I kept this savage beast,
What wreckage would it do?

Whew! It was a dream!
I thought it looked so real!
It was so petrifying,
I ought to have a meal.

My legs propelled me forward
And I pulled my mum astray,
I told her the story from beginning to end,
It took quite a while to say.

"It's alright!" she reassured me,
I knew what that was supposed to mean,

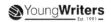

What goes on in my child's head all day?
I don't understand that dream!

So readers, there you have it,
Even if you think it's true, like me,
Don't think the dangers in your head are real,
Just know... ooh! What's that I see?

I picked it up tenderly
And hid it behind me,
I raced back to my room
And crouched on my bed to see.

Sarcastically I pondered,
What on earth it could be,
I thought and thought
About my dream and me.

It is a soft toy griffin
But how could this be?
That I saw the griffin
That nobody else could see?

My question goes unanswered
Many others do too,

But your imagination is unique
Along with you.

## Ihinosen Eboreime (9)
St Thomas Of Canterbury Catholic Primary School, Mitcham

# It's Christmas Again

All welcome, welcome,
Welcome again,
All in the town square,
Went the Christmas shoppers.
"Forward to that shop!"
"Charge for the shop!" they said.
Into the valley of shops
Went the Christmas shoppers.

Forward to the next shop,
Was anyone dismayed at the price?
The shoppers knew there was a thief
But the thief blundered.
They didn't make a reply.
There's is not the reason why,
They're just there to shop til they drop
Into the valley of shops
Went the Christmas shoppers.

Shop to the right of them,
Shop to the left of them,
Shop in front of them,

Sales and no sales,
50% with a further reduction,
Into the valley of shops,
Into the kingdom of shops,
Went the Christmas shoppers.

## Chad-William Morris (10)
St Thomas Of Canterbury Catholic Primary School, Mitcham

# Francesca

On Christmas, I excitedly tore the wrapping paper
To see an egg, which looked like…
A Baby Hatchimal,
So I took the creature into my room
And I hatched it,
I pecked the shape of a heart out.

## Francesca Marziano (9)
St Thomas Of Canterbury Catholic Primary School, Mitcham

# Our Universe

Uranus is the seventh planet of our solar system, it's the third largest and it's tilted
Neptune is the eighth planet in the solar system and it is the coldest and largest
Ixion looks like the moon, it's a dwarf planet as well
Venus is the second largest planet and also the hottest. Also known as the ancient Roman goddess of love and beauty
Earth is our home. It's the third planet and has lots of colours
Rhea is the second largest moon of Saturn, the closest moon is Titan
Saturn has rings, it's the sixth planet too
Everything is in the universe!

## Harvey Kirk-Smith (7)
Upton Meadows Primary School, Upton

# Galaxy Ap

In the distance in space where the planets are,
The planets are fantastic, shiny and precious,
The glistening planets are powerful,
They have power, they are beautiful,
They sparkle and twinkle through the night,
The planets are in the galaxy,
They are amazing,
They are so colourful,
You can't see them but they are fantastic,
Planets are amazing,
They don't stop shining, they are glistening.

## Nehal Ba Omar (7)
Upton Meadows Primary School, Upton

# Alien

**A** n alien was in a spaceship
**L** eaning towards the planet the alien crash-landed
**I** t saw some craters and fell in one
**E** ven if the alien was scared he tried not to be
**N** ever again will the alien crash-land!

## Kira Newton (7)
Upton Meadows Primary School, Upton

# Space

The moon is bright
The stars shine every night
There are 8 planets in space
They are all very ace!
And I know one thing...
Space is amazing!

**Dexter Scott (7)**
Upton Meadows Primary School, Upton

# Seasons

In summer, the sun is hot and light,
Beating down on the people so bright,
Children like to dance and play,
Lucky parents get to sunbathe all day.

In autumn, the animals go to bed,
Making their nests with leaves that are red,
Pumpkins are carved and costumes are made,
Treats and tricks are given and played.

In winter, the snow falls on the path.
So when people walk they smile and they laugh,
Carol singers come knocking at doors,
Spreading Christmas spirit with musical chords.

In spring, flowers open and bloom,
Insects buzz and birds twitter a tune,
New life begins, the circle goes round,
As one season dies, another is found.

**Anouk Palmer-Moenks (11)**
Whitehall Primary School, Whitehall

# Snowboarding

On top of the mountain,
I am feeling quite tense,
And I am getting ready for my descent,
I start off all gentle on the snow,
Then it gets steeper and off I go,
I'm as fast as a rocket,
Zooming so fast,
Then I see something that makes me gasp,
A jump;
As big as a tree,
And all the snowboarders are looking at me,
A few feet away,
There's no turning back,
But then I hear something that makes me look back,
A snowboarder that did a jump,
But failed miserably and landed in a hump.
Time suddenly slows
I don't know what to do,
Then I went off and
Suddenly flew!

I flew so far
(And this was faster than a car)
I finally did it.
I made the jump,
Then I looked around,
And it made me bump,
Everyone was clapping,
Cheering me on,
Then I stood up and I was gone,
Carving down to the bottom of the slope,
Next time, even better I hope!

## Freddie Liew (11)
Whitehall Primary School, Whitehall

# I Am Crab

I am Crab, who is wonderful,
I have a shell which is red,
I have a protected body,
Unlike cousin Hermit who is dead.

I am Crab, who is lovely,
I have to live in a pool of rocks,
I have an amazing shelter,
Unlike Spider Crab attacked by birds in flocks.

I am Crab, who is great,
I have giant, powerful claws,
I have two which I know how to use,
Unlike baby Eugene who faced a shark's jaws.

I am Crab, who is cool,
I have faster legs than most,
I have the ability to run away,
Unlike Uncle Ghost who arrived by post.

I am Crab, who is alive,
I have power to fight a lot of things,

I have lived for 4 years
Unlike all my other siblings.

## Hamid Rana (11)
Whitehall Primary School, Whitehall

# Drops Of Water

Why are we here?
Just to suffer.
We all came this way,
Just to see,
This monstrosity,
You
Could
Call
A
Human.
It was obvious,
He had been shot,
Many times,
All over.
As the crimson red liquid
Flowed out of his temple,
I could see my reflection,
And I can't lie,
I looked good in that blood.
In his blood.
It was a shame that he had to die,

But my thirst
Became too much to bear,
It was a shame,
They all had to die.
I then looked around,
At all the bodies
In the field,
It was as if everybody
Was a drop of water
To quench my thirst,
But
I would never
Have enough.

## Solomon Endersby-King (11)
Whitehall Primary School, Whitehall

# World Ending

The world has turned bad,
It's a place of trouble,
All thanks to humans,
This world's in a muddle.

It used to be a good world,
A happy world,
A new world,
But now it's a sad world,
A bad world,
Our true world.

Many people think,
If we had a new world,
We would make it happy,
I hope realisation
Will be short and snappy.

We will spread,
We will live
Throughout the universe,
All will crumble and die,
There is no turning back,

It is close,
Coming
Nearer...

## Lottie Nava (10)
Whitehall Primary School, Whitehall

# The Jam Sandwich Competition

There once was a competition
Where your mission
Was to use the English language
To help robots make a jam sandwich
Team one led
When it came to the bread
But there was a clutter
When it came to the butter
They lost the plan
When they opened the jam
So they soon go passed
By team two in the last
Two took the lead
Fuelled by their need
For the winning prize - a loaf of bread
As heavy as lead
But then... it flew off,
A flock of pigeons holding it aloft.

**Harri Snow (10)**
Whitehall Primary School, Whitehall

# Pet Dinosaurs

I have a Diplodocus and it smells like jelly
It's so big you can bounce on its belly
It can fly and it eats so much pie
And its eyes are as big as tellies.

I have a big T-Rex, her name is Georgina
She lives in the ocean and has suntan lotion
She can swim and she is thin
Because she refuses to eat.

I have a pet Triceratops, it can teleport
And is stronger than a robot
It eats mayonnaise and it stars in some plays
But it has a coat made of paper.

**Nathaniel Tsegaye (11)**
Whitehall Primary School, Whitehall

# A Day In The Life Of Ludo, My Dog

Ludo opens his eyes
Dashes in the garden
Does his business
Finds his cork
Plays
Chews his cork
And sleeps.

Ludo opens his eyes
Dashing in the garden
Does his business
Kills his toy
Plays
Eats
And sleeps.

Ludo opens his eyes
Runs in the garden
Comes inside
Gets ready to go to the

Market
Gets back
Sleeps.

Ludo opens his eyes
Eats
Plays for a bit
And sleeps.

## Fern Rockett (10)
Whitehall Primary School, Whitehall

# I Wish

I wish that the world was in peace
Where everyone was kind
Where everyone took care of the Earth
Where racism was in nobody's mind.

I wish that pollution didn't exist
And everyone would recycle
Where animals could be safe forever
Instead of driving, they'd cycle.

I wish everyone could get along
And everyone lived in harmony
Where no animals were hunted by poachers
And everyone would plant a tree.

**Ali Tariq (10)**
Whitehall Primary School, Whitehall

# Space Pandas

With their stripy faces and their optical bodies,
Their chubby cheeks that are very big
They've got scruffy arms
And they roll around
You'll get really unlucky if you get near them
And if you get near them
You won't be happy
Because you'll turn into one
And you'll have to eat bamboo
And roll around and around and around...
I think I'm going to be sick!

**Louis Parsons (11) & Bobby**
Whitehall Primary School, Whitehall

# The Soul Sucker

It creeps around the door,
Under the stairs,
In your bed,
In the middle of the night,
It sucks your soul right into it,
Leaves you
Gasping,
Struggling,
Returns to hiding.
It creeps around the door,
Under the stairs,
In your bed,
Whoever sees it,
Never ever
Sees it again,
The soul sucker...
It's right behind you!

**Aiesha Wilkinson (10)**
Whitehall Primary School, Whitehall

# My Bird Gucci

My bird Gucci is a parakeet,
She's small, young and loves to fly free
She's red, yellow, blue and green,
She is the prettiest bird I have ever seen.

She's elegant as she flies through the room,
As soon as she leaves her cage,
She immediately zooms,
I really love my bird Gucci
And in my opinion, you should agree.

**Alyssa Daveridge (11)**
Whitehall Primary School, Whitehall

# Angel Delight

My mum wakes up
Waters the plants
Makes a cup of tea
Wakes me and Charlie up
Has breakfast
Gets dressed
Goes to work.

My mum wakes up
Feeds the guinea pig
Makes packed lunches
Has breakfast
And sleeps.

My mum wakes up
We watch TV and have a snuggle
Have breakfast
I love you, Mum.

**Nicole Jacquens (10)**
Whitehall Primary School, Whitehall

# Charlie Lives On

Charlie the dog
Died last August
He slipped away
With a gentle gust
I'm sorry to say
He passed away
My dad even cried that day
I wish he was here
I wish I could see him
I wish I could borrow him back from the dead
At least for a day
To wipe my sorrow away
But he still lives on
He lives in me.

## Scarlett-May Gilpin Stone (11)
Whitehall Primary School, Whitehall

# Beautiful Butterfly

Beautiful butterfly
Flies right past
I think she must be
Having a blast.

Beautiful butterfly
Goes to see a friend
And it seems as though
Her journey will never end.

Beautiful butterfly
Flies to me
Beautiful butterfly
Fills me with glee.

Beautiful butterfly.

**Méabh Maguire (10)**
Whitehall Primary School, Whitehall

# Bully

Bully, bully, bully
Why do you have to be so rude?

Bad
Understanding how to
Learn to be nice and
Let people live a good life
You'll hurt people's feelings if you carry on
Be nice
Be caring
Bully, bully, bully
We will understand
If you tell us
We can make it work!

## Amara Grandison (11)
Whitehall Primary School, Whitehall

# Big, Black Hole

Stay away
Keep to moon and Mars
If you go to the big, black hole
You could get sucked up to a parallel universe
Not even a scientist knows
No one knows
Not if you give up your life
People have tried but ran out of air
Right at the last chime
Don't try
You'll just die.

## Elena Olsen (11)
Whitehall Primary School, Whitehall

# Dustyyyyyy!

Dustin the dog wakes up
Then lies
D
O
W
N
He wags his tail and...
runs to the door
and *barks* at an invisible cat
He goes on a walk
to the park with a lake
and *barks* at the swans
Then he goes home to sleep
*ZZZZZ!*

## Elsa Roberton (11)
Whitehall Primary School, Whitehall

# Bella!

Bella was my cat
Until of course
She went
She licked a puddle
And never came back
I'm sad of course
She got poisoned
But what could I do?
Nothing
I wish I could
But no
Why her
And now she's gone
At least I got to say goodbye.

**Iona Weaver-Brown (11)**
Whitehall Primary School, Whitehall

# Thank You

Thank you for the books I read,
Thank you for the books I need,
Whether I want to lie in the shimmering sun,
Or trek through the freezing cold mountains,
Venture through stormy seas,
Whilst exploring week by week,
Thanks for the books on my bookshelf.

## Samira Hared (10)
Whitehall Primary School, Whitehall

# Football

F ootball is fun
O h the crowd was shouting
O utstanding applause
T alking and shouting, yeah!
B all is amazing
A mazing football
L ots of people cheering
L ots of people shouting.

**Imran Mohamed (10)**
Whitehall Primary School, Whitehall

# School Is Super Fun

**S** tuff is fun at school
**C** ool learning
**H** ow fun school is, it's out of this world
**O** oh we have pet chicks in Year 1
**O** r you can play in the humungous playground
**L** ove school, it is fun!

**Jude Jennings (10)**
Whitehall Primary School, Whitehall

# Sneaky Cat

Sneaky cat,
He is not fat,
He doesn't hunt rats,
He only hunts mice,
And he can't eat rice,
Loves to cuddles
He comes to my room,
Miaows till I move
And loves to snooze,
Simba, my cat.

**Riya Juttla (10)**
Whitehall Primary School, Whitehall

# A Letter To The Moon

Dear Moon,

Don't worry my friend I'll come to you soon.
Let me tell you what I did,
Whilst being such a normal kid,
My birthday was just last week,
And I got many boring antiques,
This month we went to the fair,
But we had to leave because of a brown bear,
This year we went to my aunt's wedding,
She looked ridiculous, her dress was made of bedding,
Yesterday, we went to the beach,
By my sister, Coco, got sucked by a leech!

Please write back so I can hear from you,
From your friend, Hugh.

**Kayden Harris (11)**
Worsley Bridge Primary School, Beckenham

# What I Saw In My Dream

What I saw in my dream was...
An alien, small but scary, cute but deadly.

What I saw in my dream was...
A planet, calm and peaceful, big and beautiful.

What I saw in my dream was...
A star shining brightly in the night,
Big and bold in the darkness.

What I saw in my dream was...
A UFO, gliding in the darkness,
Buzzing all around.

What I saw in my dream was...
Space!

**Amelia Butterly (10)**
Worsley Bridge Primary School, Beckenham

# Being Kind

Bullying hurts and is unkind,
They sometimes find friends hard to find.
Everyone should try to get along
And all try to sing the same song,
Respect and kindness go along way,
With every single passing day,
So smile, be happy and be kind to each other,
After all, we are all someone's son, daughter, sister or brother.

## Caiden Walker (8)
Worsley Bridge Primary School, Beckenham

# Space

S tars like diamonds, dancing in the darkness
P lanets orbit and twirl around the blazing sun
A steroids bolt through the blackness, rapid flames crackling
C osmic rocketships, zooming through the magical world,
E arth, oh brilliant Earth, the planet full of life.

## Naomi Francis
Worsley Bridge Primary School, Beckenham

# YOUNG WRITERS INFORMATION

We hope you have enjoyed reading this book – and that you will continue to in the coming years.

If you're a young writer who enjoys reading and creative writing, or the parent of an enthusiastic poet or story writer, do visit our website **www.youngwriters.co.uk**. Here you will find free competitions, workshops and games, as well as recommended reads, a poetry glossary and our blog. There's lots to keep budding writers motivated to write!

If you would like to order further copies of this book, or any of our other titles, then please give us a call or order via your online account.

Young Writers
Remus House
Coltsfoot Drive
Peterborough
PE2 9BF
(01733) 890066
info@youngwriters.co.uk

Join in the conversation!
Tips, news, giveaways and much more!

 YoungWritersUK     @YoungWritersCW